MAKE ME LAUGH!

ANIMAL ANTICS

THE BEAST JOKES EVER

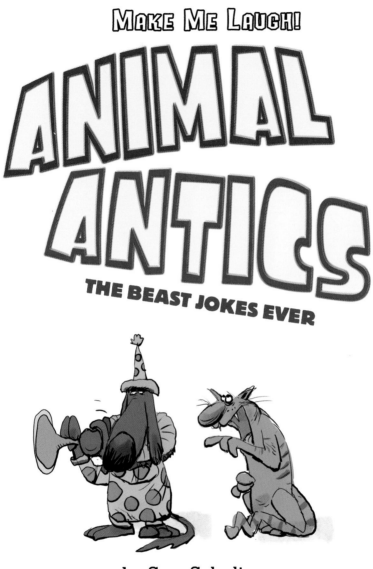

by Sam Schultz
pictures by Brian Gable

Carolrhoda Books, Inc. • Minneapolis

Danny: Our new dog is like one of the family.

Ellie: Yes, I can see the resemblance!

Q: What side of a cat has the most fur?

A: The outside.

Q: Why does your pet owl go "Tweet, tweet"?

A: Because she doesn't give a hoot!

Kerry: We just sold our Thoroughbred horse for $100.

Sherry: We just sold our purebred fox terrier.

Kerry: What did you sell him for?

Sherry: For wetting on the carpet!

Q: What can a cat have that dogs can't have?

A: Kittens.

Two fleas came out of a movie theater. They saw it was raining outside. One flea said to the other, "Do you want to walk, or should we take a dog?"

First Dog: My master calls me "Tootsie." What does your master call you?

Second Dog: He calls me "Sitboy!"

Dylan: Wow, that dolphin trainer never makes mistakes!

Derek: Nope—she does everything on porpoise!

Q: How can you keep a goat from smelling?

A: Plug his nose!

Eye Doctor: What seems to be the trouble?

Leopard Trainer: I don't know. I keep seeing spots before my eyes!

Mark: My dog sleeps with me at night.

Susie: Ugh, that's not healthy!

Mark: I know, but he doesn't mind.

Q: What can an elephant have that a flea can't have?

A: An elephant can have fleas, but a flea can't have elephants!

Q: Why does your dog always scratch herself in the same spot?

A: Because that's where she itches!

Father Kangaroo: Why are you spanking Junior?

Mother Kangaroo: Because he's been eating crackers in bed.

Q: What's big and red and hides behind a tree?

A: An embarrassed elephant.

First Snake: I sure hope I'm not poisonous!

Second Snake: Why?

First Snake: Because I just bit my tongue!

Lady Customer: I'd like a pair of alligator shoes.

Salesman: Of course, miss. What size is your alligator?

Q: Who do you feel more sorry for—a dog or a cat?

A: A cat. Because cats are such purr things.

Q: What do dogs and trees have in common?

A: Their bark.

Amy: Hey, your dog just bit my ankle.

Jamie: What did you expect? She's just a small dog, and she can't reach any higher!

Debbie: If I say, "Come here, Rover," will your dog come to me?

Dirk: Nope.

Debbie: Why not?

Dirk: Because his name is Fido!

Q: What is the best way to hide in the desert?

A: Wear camel-flauge.

Q: When is the best time to take your pet lion for a walk?

A: Any time he wants to go!

Tiger Cub: Look, Mom, I'm chasing a hunter around a tree!

Mother Tiger: How many times must I tell you not to play with your food?

Rodney: Did you know an elephant never forgets?

Vanessa: Big deal! What does he have to remember?

Teacher: Susie, name four members of the cat family.

Susie: Mother, father, sister, and brother.

Veterinarian: Has your cat ever had any fleas?

Cat Owner: No, just kittens.

Q: What should you do when a bull charges you?

A: Pay him!

Dan: My parents just bought me a bird for a pet.

Jan: What kind is it?

Dan: A keet.

Jan: You mean a parakeet.

Dan: No, they only bought me one.

Q: Why are elephants ashamed to go to the beach?

A: Because they have a hard time keeping their trunks up!

Hank: I took my dog to a movie yesterday, but she didn't want to stay.

Frank: Why not?

Hank: She thought the book was better!

Q: What did one old firefly say to the other?

A: "Your grandson sure is bright for his age!"

Katie: My mother can't stand my pet duck.

Kerry: Why not?

Katie: She's a wise quacker.

Mr. Johnson: I can't get my police dog to open his mouth. You'd better get over here quick!

Policeman: Mister, you don't want the police. You want a veterinarian.

Mr. Johnson: No, I want the police. I can't get him to open his mouth because he has a burglar in it!

Q: What kind of a dog would a person bite?

A: A hot dog!

Ethan: What happened to you?

Emily: I fell while I was riding.

Ethan: Horseback?

Emily: I don't know. I'll find out when I get back to the stable!

Q: What do you get when an elephant bumps into a cherry tree?

A: A cherry shake!

Q: Why do elephants travel in groups?

A: Because group rates are cheaper!

Q: Why is a dog a man's best friend?

A: Because he wags his tail instead of his tongue.

Q: Why didn't the owners of a lost dog advertise for her in the paper?

A: Because the dog couldn't read.

Arnie: My dog tried to arrest me for crossing the street against the light.

Annie: You mean he tried to stop you from crossing the street.

Arnie: No, he tried to arrest me. He's a police dog.

Harry: I have a pet mouse that squeaks all day.

Larry: Why don't you try oiling it?

Peter: I've got a cat who can say its own name!

Karen: That's great! What's your cat's name?

Peter: "Meow."

Ron: A bear ran through our camp last week, and our camp leader shot the bear in his pajamas.

Don: No way. Bears don't wear pajamas!

Teacher: If this statue came to life, what do you think it would say?

Student: "Anybody want a pet pigeon?"

Mother: Willy, I thought I told you not to teach your parrot any bad words!

Willy: I'm not, Mom. I'm just telling him what he's not supposed to say!

Q: Why do cats look larger at night than in the morning?

A: Because they're usually let out at night and taken in in the morning.

Teacher: How do you spell leopard?

Student: L-E-P-A-R-D.

Teacher: The dictionary spells it L-E-O-P-A-R-D.

Student: But you asked me how I spell it!

Q: What's a monkey's favorite month?

A: Ape-ril.

Q: What would you get if you crossed a canary with a cat?

A: A peeping tom.

Woman: When you sold me this cat, you promised me it would be good for mice.

Clerk: Isn't it?

Woman: It hasn't caught a mouse since I've had it.

Clerk: Isn't that good for mice?

Q: What kind of dog hands out tickets?

A: A police dog.

Q: What kind of sharks never eat women?

A: Man-eating sharks!

Q: Why can't rabbits go bald?

A: Because they keep producing hares.

Jack: My dog is worth $500.

Mack: How can a dog save that much money?

Mother: Billy, why did you pull the cat's tail?

Billy: I didn't pull her tail, Mother. I was standing on it, and she pulled it.

Barry: We have a new dog!

Terry: What's she like?

Barry: Anything we feed her!

Q: What was the elephant doing on the freeway?

A: About five miles per hour!

Will: I've got an alligator named Ginger.

Jill: Does Ginger bite?

Will: No, Ginger snaps.

First Leopard: Well, how did you enjoy dinner?

Second Leopard: It sure hit the spots!

First Cow: I just can't get over what I saw last night.

Second Cow: What was it?

First Cow: The moon.

Cat: My master gets a kick out of me.

Dog: When my master tries that, he gets a bite out of me!

Game Warden: Young man, it's against the law to fish in this lake!

Young Man: Oh, I'm not fishing, sir. I'm just teaching my pet worm how to swim!

Q: Why do elephants always have wrinkles?

A: Because they're too big to iron out.

Brian: Boy, I sure wish I had a pet giraffe.

Ryan: How come?

Brian: I can't reach the peanut butter!

Two kangaroos were walking through the park. One kangaroo asked the other where her son was. She looked down at her empty pouch and screamed, "Help! My pocket's been picked!"

Q: Why does your cat make such an awful noise at night?

A: Ever since she ate the canary, she thinks she can sing!

Mother: Why are you crying?

Little Girl: Because I wanted to get a dog for my new baby brother.

Mother: Well, that's no reason to cry.

Little Girl: Yes it is! Nobody would trade me!

Q: Why do hummingbirds hum?

A: Because they don't know the words!

Q: Why did the elephant quit the circus?

A: He didn't want to work for peanuts anymore.

Jenny: I just bought five ducks and five pounds of cheese.

Benny: What for?

Jenny: Because I like cheese and quackers!

Mrs. Jones: Why does your son always say "Cluck, cluck, cluck"?

Mrs. Smith: Because he thinks he's a chicken.

Mrs. Jones: Why don't you tell him he's not a chicken?

Mrs. Smith: Because we need the eggs!

Jimmy: I've got a pet pig named Ball Point.

Timmy: Ball Point? That's a funny name for a pig.

Jimmy: That's her pen name.

Georgie: Yesterday I came face to face with a lion!

Porgie: Weren't you scared?

Georgie: Naw. I just turned away and walked past his cage.

Q: Why don't animals make good dancers?

A: Because they have two left feet!

Jack: I'd like some birdseed, please.

Pet Store Clerk: How many birds do you have?

Jack: None. I want to grow some!

Q: Why did the farmer put bells on his cow?

A: Because the horns didn't work.

Q: What is cowhide used for?

A: To hold the cow together.

Q: Why did the man count elephants in his sleep instead of sheep?

A: Because he was nearsighted.

Q: What sounds worse than a cat up a tree?

A: Two cats up a tree.

Barry: How do you catch a unique rabbit?

Bessie: You 'neak up on it.

Barry: How do you catch a tame rabbit?

Bessie: Tame way—you 'neak up on it.

Q: What did the mother skunk tell her son after she gave him a chemistry set?

A: "Now don't smell up the house."

Billy: I just saw a man-eating shark.

Willy: Where?

Billy: In a restaurant!

Little Worm: Am I late, Mother?

Mother Worm: Yes! Where in earth have you been?

First Boy: I can't talk to you while my goat is nearby.

Second Boy: Why not?

First Boy: Because she always butts in.

Q: What does a skunk do when it's angry?

A: Raises a stink.

Polly: How do you know ants are smart?

Molly: Because they always seem to know when we're having a picnic.

Betsy: I'd like some booties for my dog's birthday.

Store Clerk: You'll have to bring your dog in to try some on.

Betsy: I can't do that! I want them to be a surprise!

Q: What kind of snake snaps at people?

A: A garter snake.

Tim: I taught my dog to play checkers.

Jim: Really? You must have a pretty smart dog.

Tim: Not that smart. I can beat her two out of three games!

Q: What did the boy say when his cat began to purr?

A: "He left his motor running!"

Davy: My dog ate my reading book.

Sally: What did you do about it?

Davy: I took the words right out of his mouth.

Q: How would you know if there's an elephant under your bed when you wake up in the morning?

A: Your nose would be touching the ceiling.

A man ran over Mrs. Smith's cat. He went to her door to apologize.

Man: I would like to replace your cat.

Mrs. Smith: Well, you'd better do it fast. There's a mouse in the kitchen!

Boy: How much are those puppies in the window?

Pet Store Man: Twenty dollars apiece.

Boy: How much is a whole one?

Q: How do you get down from an elephant?

A: You don't. You get down from a goose.

Q: How many elephants can you fit in a Volkswagen bug?

A: Five. Two in front, two in back, and one in the glove compartment!

Mailman: Your dog bit my leg!

Woman: Did you put anything on it?

Mailman: No, he seemed to like it just the way it was.

Q: Why do puppies make better pets than elephants?

A: Try taking an elephant to bed with you and you'll soon find out!

Q: What kind of cat hangs around a bowling alley?

A: An alley cat.

Q: What's the difference between an elephant and a mouse?

A: About 5,000 pounds.

Jack: I got a cow for my birthday.

Jane: Does it give milk?

Jack: No, I have to take it from her.

Joey: My dog Ossie is sick, so we're taking him to an animal doctor.

Moey: Gee, I thought all doctors were people!

Q: What did the woman say when her dog ran away?

A: Doggone-it!

Pet Store Owner: Yes, I have a singing cat and mouse for sale.

Buyer: Do they really sing?

Pet Store Owner: Well, to tell you the truth, the cat is a ventriloquist!

Q: What does a rabbit use to comb its fur?

A: A harebrush.

This book is available in two editions:
Library binding by Carolrhoda Books, Inc.,
  a division of Lerner Publishing Group
Soft cover by First Avenue Editions,
  an imprint of Lerner Publishing Group
241 First Avenue North
Minneapolis, MN 55401 U.S.A.

Website address: www.carolrhodabooks.com

Library of Congress Cataloging-in-Publication Data

Schultz, Sam.
    Animal antics: the beast jokes ever! / by Sam Schultz ; illustrations by Brian Gable.
       p.   cm. — (Make me laugh)
    Summary: A collection of jokes and riddles about all kinds of animals.
    ISBN: 1–57505–640–2 (lib. bdg. : alk. paper)
    ISBN: 1–57505–702–6 (pbk. : alk. paper)
    1. Animals—Juvenile humor. [1. Animals—Humor. 2. Jokes. 3. Riddles.]
    I. Title. II. Series.
    PN6231.A5 S33 2004
    818'.5402—dc21   2002011835

Manufactured in the United States of America
2 3 4 5 6 7 – DP – 09 08 07 06 05 04